MAXINE B. ROSENBERG

Brothers and Sisters

photographs by
GEORGE ANCONA

CLARION BOOKS · NEW YORK

To Maeva and Susan,

two sisters who are like sisters to me—M.R.

To Lisa—G.A.

Book design by Vicky Hartman

Photographs on pages 5 & 8 by Maxine Rosenberg.

Clarion Books
a Houghton Mifflin Company imprint
215 Park Avenue South, New York, NY 10003
Text copyright © 1991 by Maxine B. Rosenberg
Photographs copyright © 1991 by George Ancona

Printed in the U.S.A.

Library of Congress Cataloging-in-Publication Data
Rosenberg, Maxine B.
Brothers and sisters/by Maxine B. Rosenberg; photographs by
George Ancona.
p. cm.
Summary: Follows the ever-changing and growing
relationships of brothers and sisters in three different families.
ISBN 0-395-51121-6
1. Brothers and sisters—Case studies—Juvenile literature.
[1. Brothers and sisters.] I. Ancona, George, ill. II. Title.
BF723.S43R67 1991
306.875'3—dc20   90-48547
                                                     CIP
                                                     AC

HOR 10 9 8 7 6 5 4 3 2 1

Introduction

Most children have at least one brother or sister. Since no two people anywhere are exactly alike, no two brothers and sisters get along the same. In one family, brothers and sisters may be kind and caring, while in another, they may bicker all the time. Usually, though, brothers and sisters are good friends who argue now and then.

How brothers and sisters feel about one another has something to do with having been born first, last, or in the middle of the family. For example, younger brothers and sisters may like the oldest or firstborn child to help them and teach them things. But if these older brothers and sisters act too bossy, the younger ones may become angry.

And while older brothers and sisters may be given special treats because of their age, they still may get jealous when the younger ones, needing closer attention, spend more time with Mommy.

Those children born in the middle are both older and younger siblings, depending on which other child in the family they are with. When they are in charge of the younger ones, they may feel very grown up. When they are cared for and protected by a big brother or sister, they may feel comforted and safe. That's why children born in the middle sometimes feel they are in the best spot of all. Yet at other times, they may feel confused about which place they really hold.

Youngest, oldest, or born somewhere in between, brothers and sisters have a special relationship. Even as they grow up and go off on their own, brothers and sisters stay friends throughout the years.

🌸 *Chapter One* 🌸

Jessica, the Oldest of Three Sisters

Last year, when Jessica was almost five, her youngest sister, Candice, was born. At that time her other sister, Lana, was three. "When Mommy was busy with the new baby, I made sure Lana didn't get into trouble. If she put a penny in her mouth, I called Mommy to come quickly and take it out.

"Now I take care of Candice, too. Sometimes when Mommy's talking on the phone, I feed the baby. Or if Mommy has work to do, I put Candice in the stroller and we go for a walk. The other day when Daddy was taking care of us, he asked me to keep an eye on the baby so he could watch a baseball game on TV. Afterward he gave me a quarter for doing such a good job. With that money I bought an extra treat in school—Hawaiian Punch."

Jessica, the oldest child in her family, likes to help out and also enjoys being in charge of her sisters. It makes her feel grown up. But Lana, who's two years younger, balks if Jessica tries to do too much for her. "You'd think Lana would be happy when I make her breakfast on the mornings Mommy and Daddy sleep late," says Jessica. "Instead of thanking me, she says, 'I want Mommy to pour my juice, not you.'

"Even when I try to teach her numbers so we can play a math game I have, she says, 'I can do it myself.' At least she doesn't fuss when we play house. She lets me be the mother, and she's the child."

Sometimes Jessica thinks that Lana, being younger, gets special treatment. "When Mommy and Daddy bought me a brand-new two wheeler and gave Lana my old tricycle, Lana was unhappy. So Mommy bought her a Big Wheel at a garage sale. Now Lana can ride faster than me because she doesn't have to get used to training wheels.

"Still, I'm glad I'm older than my two sisters. I can do a lot of stuff they can't. I can read, swim without a bubble, and do somersaults in gymnastics. Lana and Candice aren't ready for those things yet. They're not even big enough to help Daddy wash the car.

"At night I get to stay up later than they do. When Uncle Toby comes over, I watch TV with him and Mommy until nine. Candice and Lana have to be in bed at seven."

Since her two sisters are around from the minute she gets off the school bus, Jessica isn't alone with her mother very often. "I have to wait until Candice is asleep before Mommy can come into my room and help me with my homework. Lana's supposed to be playing by herself then. But instead she opens my door and pretends she has a school question, too. If Mommy tells her to leave, she gets mad.

"It's not always fun having two younger sisters. Either Candice is pulling the toys off my shelf, or Lana forgets to put the caps back on my markers. I like them both anyway, and I'm nice to them. Every night I read Candice bedtime stories. And the other day I let Lana wear my favorite necklace.

"Besides, I like having them around to play with. I'd rather set up my dollhouse furniture with Lana than do it by myself."

Early in the morning Lana comes into Jessica's room to watch television with her. Recently Lana spilled milk on Jessica's new rug. "When Mommy asked who did it, Lana and I were both quiet. I didn't want my sister to get punished. But Mommy found out the truth anyhow and sent Lana to her room. When I heard my sister crying, I went in and hugged her.

"Last week my friend Melissa was visiting, and she acted mean to Lana. I told Melissa, 'If you can't be nice to my sister, you'll have to go back to your own house,' so Melissa stopped. She knows that Lana and I stick up for each other.

"And my sister and I help each other too. In the park, we take turns on the swings. I'll push her, and then she'll push me.

"When we're older, Lana and I are going to talk on the phone all the time. If she needs her clothes shortened, I'll tell her to come to my house, and I'll sew them for her the way Mommy fixes Uncle Toby's things. Maybe I'll ask her to stay for dinner. While I cook, she can set the table.

"Probably we'll work together, too. I'm not sure if I'll be a vet or make pizzas, but either way, I'll give Lana a job so we can be near each other."

❧ Chapter Two ❧

Justin, the Youngest in His Family

When Justin's older brother, Brian, started school, Justin waved goodbye to him as the bus took off. Suddenly he turned to his mother and cried, "I don't want to stay home without Brian. He's my friend."

From the time Justin was born, he's always had a brother who plays with him and protects him. "If I fall down and get a bloody knee, Brian picks me up and takes me into the house. He calls Mommy to hurry and bring me a bandage. I can tell he's sad that I'm hurt.

"Even when I get yelled at for throwing my toys around, Brian feels badly for me. He gives me a hug and sometimes a piece of candy."

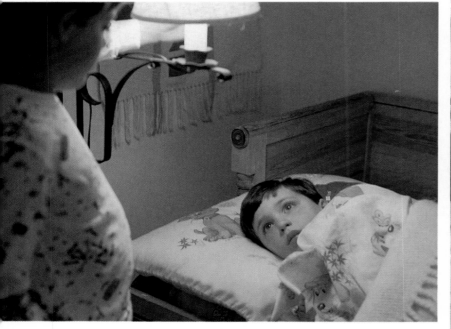

At night Justin's afraid to sleep in the dark, although there's a tiny light plugged into the wall. "That little night-light is too far away from my bed, and I can't work the lamp switch right near me. So I ask Brian to turn it on, and he does. My brother's really nice.

"Once in a while, if I tiptoe into his room and tell him I've had a bad dream, he lets me sleep with him. But if I move around too much, he makes me go out. I wish I could move my bed in next to his, but I don't think he'd like that."

Justin's glad he has an older brother who is both comforting at night and fun to play with. Although Justin has lots of friends his own age, he prefers being with Brian. "We get on our swing set and throw ropes to each other to make believe we're Indiana Jones in the jungle. If Brian needs to scout for enemies, I help him get on the top of the bar.

"Indoors, we mostly play with my hot dog stand. Usually I sell Brian the toy food, and he pretends to eat it. It's a good game unless Brian says he wants to be the boss and I should be the customer. 'Forget it,' I tell him, 'I'll play alone.' Then I take the toy away. If Mommy hears us shouting, she makes us go to our rooms. The minute she leaves, I sneak out to play with Brian again."

Most often Brian's the one who decides what game the two will play, and Justin's happy to follow. But when it comes to sharing his toys, Justin wants to be in charge. And that sometimes leads to arguments. "If I feel like it, I'll let Brian use my plastic typewriter, but if I don't, I tell him not to touch it. Then Brian says to me, 'Who cares!'"

Since Justin is only four and a half, he has fewer chores than his older brother. "Both of us put our toys and bikes away, but Brian has to set and clear the table too, and he has lots of homework to do at night. Also he has to baby-sit me when Mommy and Daddy go for a walk. I like when he does that, unless he wants to read to me. I won't let him, because he says the words too slowly."

For the most part, Justin's happy about being the youngest child, although at times he wishes he were as grown up as his older brother. "Brian plays soccer every Saturday. When Daddy and I take him to the game, Brian lets me wear his old uniform. But I'm too young to join the team.

"And only Brian gets invited to his friends' birthday parties, even though I play with those kids when they come to our house. Mommy knows I'm sad when we drop Brian off at the party. She takes me to the store and buys me an ice cream cone, but still I'd rather be with the big guys."

Being the youngest is especially hard for Justin when Brian talks about school. "If my brother brags about the new words and hard math he's learned in first grade, Mommy and Daddy say, 'Wonderful.' When I tell them that Samantha fell off the chair in nursery school, they just say, 'Oh.'

"Last year Brian started taking violin lessons, but Mommy said I wasn't ready. At the recital, I watched Brian play on stage and told Mommy again that I wanted to play the violin. She said, 'We'll see.'

"Now I have a violin teacher too, just like Brian. I practice all the time, but I have trouble putting my fingers on the right string. So Brian shows me what to do.

"The other day I said to him, 'Brian, you're my best friend.' And Brian said to me, 'You're my best friend too.'"

❧ *Chapter Three* ❧

Joseph, in the Middle

Of my two sisters, Lavinia Rose is the one I like playing with the most. Even though she's only three and I'm six, we get along because she usually shares her things.

"For some reason, I have lots of fights with Olusola (pronounced O-lu-sho-la), my older sister who's seven. Even so, I think she's very kind. When I'm sick and have to stay home from school, she helps me with the stuff I've missed. If I forget how a letter looks, she holds my hand and writes it out with me."

Growing up between two sisters, Joseph has always had someone to keep him company. "When I'm outdoors and want to have
a bike race or a game of kickball, I ask Oluṣola. She's good in
sports, so we have fun.

"But indoors, I play more with Lavinia Rose because we like to
pretend. Once in a while, though, Lavinia Rose grabs what I'm
using and won't let go. I don't like it when she does that."

Still, Joseph protects his younger sister, and this makes him
feel good. "Sometimes when Oluṣola and I are playing, Lavinia
Rose comes into the room. Oluṣola says to her, 'Get out, this
minute!' I tell Oluṣola, 'Don't be mean to our baby sister. She's
just a little kid.' And Oluṣola listens.

26

"I like helping Lavinia Rose. If she hurts herself and starts crying, I hold her and pat her back. But Lavinia Rose can be pretty pesty, like when she messes up the Bingo game after I've taken so long to match the numbers on my card. Even then I try to be nice to her, but it's hard. Having a younger sister means there's always someone to bother me."

Joseph feels that because Lavinia Rose is the youngest, she gets away with too much. "Everyone in our house has chores, except Lavinia Rose. When Mommy asked me which two I wanted, I picked washing the tub and vacuuming. Lavinia Rose didn't have to choose a chore. She could at least take turns with Olusọla and me setting the table, but Mommy says she's too young. That makes me mad.

"As the baby, Lavinia Rose gets to do lots of things alone with Mommy. And Oluṣọla, being the oldest, goes with Daddy to the diner for supper or with Mommy to the high school to see a show. I try not to care, but I wish I could go too.

"Still, I'm pretty lucky, being in the middle. My parents do special things with me too. When I behave the best in church, Mommy takes only me out for dinner. And Daddy teaches me football because he knows that when I grow up, I want to play the game professionally. Last week he started giving me organ lessons because I told him I was interested in learning to play."

It bothers Joseph when Oluṣọla, who is only a year older, treats him like a baby. "On the days Mommy gives violin lessons, Oluṣọla and I are both in charge of Lavinia Rose. Usually we manage together okay, except if Oluṣọla gets mad at me and sends me to my room. I say to her, 'No way, José.'

"Other times she invites her friends over, and then she shuts her bedroom door. She says that girls don't like playing house with boys. But when my friend Sarah visits, I let Oluṣọla and Lavinia Rose build bridges with us."

Most afternoons when they get off the bus, Olụṣọla and Joseph play together. "I'm very nice to my sister, especially when she tells me about a kid in class who was mean to her. I say, 'Olụṣọla, don't be sad. I like you.'

"Sometimes, though, I wish I had a brother so I wouldn't be the only boy in the family. Then the girls could go off by themselves, while my brother and I could toss a football around."

Nevertheless Joseph is glad that Lavinia Rose and Olụṣọla are his sisters. "I told Olụṣọla that when we're grown up, we should live together. Then if she had to rush someplace, I could fix her dinner, the way Daddy helps Mommy out. With the two of us in the same house, we'd take care of each other. That way I'd always feel safe.

"And I'd have company all the time."